Let Freedom Ring

Tecumseh

Shawnee Leader

by Susan R. Gregson

Consultant:
Dr. Larry L. Nelson, Site Manager
Fort Meigs State Memorial
Ohio Historical Society
Perrysburg, Ohio

Bridgestone Books
an imprint of Capstone Press
Mankato, Minnesota

Bridgestone Books are published by Capstone Press
151 Good Counsel Drive, P.O. Box 669, Mankato, Minnesota 56002
http://www.capstone-press.com

Library of Congress Cataloging-in-Publication Data
Gregson, Susan R.
    Tecumseh : Shawnee leader/by Susan R. Gregson.
        p. cm. — (Let freedom ring)
    Summary: Traces the life of the Shawnee Indian leader, including his struggle to regain lost Indian territory, his efforts to unite American Indian nations, and his death during the War of 1812.
    Includes bibliographical references and index.
    ISBN 0-7368-1556-2 (hardcover)
    1. Tecumseh, Shawnee Chief, 1768–1813—Juvenile literature. 2. Shawnee Indians—Biography—Juvenile literature. 3. Indians of North America—Government relations—Juvenile literature. [1. Tecumseh, Shawnee chief, 1768–1813. 2. Shawnee Indians—Biography. 3. Indians of North America—Biography. 4. Kings, queens, rulers, etc.] I. Title. II. Series.
E99.S35 T149 2003
977'.004973'0092—dc21   2002012004

Editorial Credits
Charles Pederson, editor; Kia Adams, series designer; Juliette Peters, book designer and illustrator; Kelly Garvin, photo researcher; Karen Risch, product planning editor

Photo Credits
Bettmann/Corbis, 12
The Felson Historical Society, Louisville, KY, cover (inset)
Library of Congress, 7, 38, 43
North Wind Picture Archives, 18–19, 24, 28, 31, 35, 42
Ohio Historical Society, cover (main), 11, 16, 21, 23
Paramount Press/Robert Griffing, 15
Reader's Digest/Used with permission from *Through Indian Eyes,* copyright 1995 by the Reader's Digest Association, Inc. Pleasantville, NY, 37
Saline County Tourism Board and American Indian Society of Southern
    Illinois/Jeptha Bright, 5
Stock Montage, Inc., 27
Susan Underwood, 9, 41

1   2   3   4   5   6   08   07   06   05   04   03

Table of Contents

Chapter One

Tecumseh the Legend

A bronze statue stands at the head of a wooded mountain trail near the Shawnee National Forest in Illinois. The statue shows the figure of Tecumseh, a chief of the Shawnee Indian people. He wears a leather shirt and leggings. In one hand, he carries a bundle of sticks. Tecumseh rode his horse from one American Indian nation to another. He asked each nation to help him keep white settlers from taking Indian land. According to legend, he said, "One stick breaks easily. But a bundle of sticks is hard to break." The tribes had to work together to be as strong as the bundle.

Tecumseh was born in present-day Ohio just before the U.S. Revolutionary War (1775–1783). He lived when American colonists first began to move west into American Indian land.

John O'Dell sculpted what Tecumseh looked like in the early 1800s. The statue, finished in 2002, stands near the Shawnee National Forest in Illinois.

Tecumseh's Name

Tecumseh's name has been spelled and pronounced in many ways. People have written it *Tekumfi, Tikumfa, Tecumtha, Tekamthi,* and *Tikomfi.* Today, the accepted way to spell his name is *Tecumseh.* It is pronounced tuh-KOOM-seh, or sometimes tuh-KOOM-see.

Tecumseh died during the War of 1812 (1812–1814), fighting to save his land from white settlement. Tecumseh was a warrior, a peacemaker, a powerful speaker, and a leader. He was brave, intelligent, fair, loyal to his people, and kind to his prisoners. Friends and many of his enemies admired him.

Stories about Tecumseh have been passed down through the years. Some stories are true, some are not. But these stories have helped to make Tecumseh a legend.

Tecumseh has been the subject of many stories. He was a powerful, brave, and fair leader of his people.

Chapter Two

Panther in the Sky

Shawnee people still tell the story of Tecumseh's birth. Shooting stars called meteors filled the night sky moments before he was born in March 1768. The name Tecumseh meant shooting star.

Shawnee babies received their names 10 to 12 days after birth. The names reflected the babies' family and a good luck charm or a special event called an unsoma. An unsoma usually represented an animal. The unsoma stayed with a Shawnee during his or her life. Tecumseh's unsoma was a panther. Tecumseh's name sometimes meant panther.

Tecumseh had a large family. His parents lived in Old Piqua, a Shawnee village on the banks of the Mad River near present-day Springfield, Ohio. They belonged to the Shawnee Panther clan. This large group of related people traced their family back to a single ancestor.

Susan Underwood painted her idea of Tecumseh's birth. A shooting star flies overhead while a panther appears to the Shawnee.

Tecumseh's father was a chief who died in battle when Tecumseh was about 6 years old. Tecumseh's mother, older brothers, and older sister raised Tecumseh. He was the fifth of seven children in the family. Lalawethika, a younger brother, later worked with Tecumseh to unite many American Indian nations.

A Leader in a Shawnee World

Tecumseh became a leader at an early age. He was a skilled, athletic hunter admired by many young Shawnee men. His older brother and sister taught him to be fair and honorable. As a teenager, he questioned the practices of the Shawnee elders. He asked them to stop the torture of captured settlers because it was cowardly. The tribe stopped torturing settlers. Although the Shawnee still killed some captured settlers, they set some free and adopted others as members of the tribe.

Tecumseh became a fearless warrior. Growing up, Tecumseh helped to raid white settlers' villages, supply boats, and hunting parties.

The Shawnee in the 1700s

The Shawnee moved from place to place along the rivers in Ohio, Indiana, Illinois and Missouri. At each place they stopped, they grew crops and ate corn, squash, pumpkins, nuts, and berries. Hunters such as the one below sometimes used a bow and arrows to hunt for meat.

The Shawnee built homes of skins and bent wood. Sometimes they built small log cabins around a large, central meetinghouse.

Families and communities relied on each other. Both men and women could be chiefs and were involved in making decisions.

As a young man, Tecumseh broke his leg hunting buffalo and had to miss many hunting trips. He once used crutches to follow his brother and other hunters. The break never properly healed, possibly because he kept hunting. Tecumseh limped slightly for the rest of his life. He walked straight, and the limp did not slow him down. Most people did not even notice it.

During the mid-1700s, the French and British armies fought against each other in the French and Indian War (1754–1763). The countries fought for

American Indians helped either the French or the British during attacks against enemies during the French and Indian War. At right, American Indians attack a French fort.

Settlers Bring Disease

White settlers and traders exposed the Indians to measles and smallpox. The Indians had not been exposed to these germs before, and their bodies could not fight the germs. Some people believe that from 1600 to 1700, such diseases killed about half of all Indians east of the Mississippi River. Indians who survived often spread the germs to tribes farther west, killing even more people.

control of the valuable fur trade in North America. Many Indian nations fought in the war. Some fought on the side of the French, some on the side of the British. The Shawnee fought alongside the British.

After Great Britain won the war, British citizens and American colonists moved in large numbers onto Shawnee hunting grounds in the Northwest Territory. This territory covered the area of present-day Ohio, Indiana, Illinois, Michigan, Wisconsin, and eastern Minnesota. The settlers' activities frightened and angered the Shawnee and other Indian nations.

Chapter Three

Tecumseh's Vanishing Land

During the Revolutionary War, President George Washington sent U.S. Army General George Rogers Clark to protect settlers. Clark's soldiers burned many Indian villages so settlers could take over the land. One of the villages was Old Piqua, Tecumseh's birthplace.

In 1783, the war ended when the United States and Great Britain signed a peace treaty. The United States turned its attention west. People wanted to explore, spread out, and conquer new territory.

White settlers forcefully took and cleared land that belonged to various American Indian nations. These settlers built villages and forts west of the Appalachian Mountains.

Robert Griffing painted Tecumseh (center) leading his followers on a journey to gather Indian allies. American Indians fought to keep their way of life separate from American settlers.

Settlers Arrive

The Shawnee and other Indian nations lived differently than U.S. settlers. The Indians in the area were mainly hunters. They believed that all land in their territory was theirs to use. White settlers were usually farmers. They claimed large areas of land to grow crops and raise animals.

Instead of sharing Indian land, settlers moved the Indians off it. Settlers put fences around the property they claimed. They believed the land belonged to individuals, not to everyone.

Under the command of General Anthony Wayne, American soldiers on horseback defeated Indians from many different nations during the Battle of Fallen Timbers.

By 1793, the Shawnee had begun to battle the United States. Tecumseh's older brother was killed in a military raid, but Indian forces won several battles against the U.S. military. President George Washington sent foot soldiers and soldiers on horseback to protect the growing settlements in the Northwest Territory.

In 1794, the Battle of Fallen Timbers was fought. General Anthony Wayne's forces met 1,300 warriors from many Indian nations for a battle near the Maumee River. Wayne's forces proved too strong for the Indians. The Shawnee and their allies retreated into nearby swamps.

The Treaty of Greenville

A year after the Battle of Fallen Timbers, Wayne and nearly 100 leaders from a dozen Indian nations signed the Treaty of Greenville. According to this agreement, the Indians gave the United States most of Ohio in exchange for $20,000 right away. The government also agreed to pay a few thousand dollars each year forever. The government paid the amount in the form of food and goods, not cash.

People of the South

The word "Shawnee" comes from the Algonquian word "sawanwa," meaning person of the south. The Shawnee tribes lived farther south than any other speakers of Algonquian languages.

The government decided how much the food and goods were worth each year. After a few years, the United States stopped making any payments.

Tecumseh did not attend the Greenville peace council. He was angry with the chiefs who signed the treaty. Little by little, the U.S. government was taking Indian land. Tecumseh began to think about uniting different tribes to save the land for all tribes.

He wanted to create a peaceful Indian alliance alongside the United States. But first, the Shawnee and others would have to stop settlers from moving west.

Over the next few years, Tecumseh visited white settlements when he hunted and traded in Ohio. He was unhappy with what he saw. Shawnee and members of other tribes drank too much alcohol. Many of Tecumseh's people were sick and weak from diseases caught from settlers and traders. White settlers were clearing large areas of land for farms. Tecumseh became even more determined to bring the tribes together.

After the Revolutionary War, many Americans entered Shawnee land to start their own farms. Tecumseh was unhappy about the movement of white people onto Shawnee land.

Chapter Four

Bringing Together a People

Tecumseh's brother Lalawethika was not like Tecumseh. He was an alcoholic who drank much of the time. His name meant "the rattle." As a boy, he was a clumsy hunter. He lost his right eye in a hunting accident.

One day in 1805, Lalawethika drank until he became unconscious. He fell into a deep coma. His family thought he was dead and prepared for his funeral. The next day, he awoke and told his friends and family that he had seen Moneto, the Master of All Life. He said that Moneto told him how to save the Indian nations from the white people. The Shawnee and other nations must give up the ways of the settlers.

Lalawethika gave up drinking alcohol. He changed his name to Tenskwatawa, meaning "open door."

Tecumseh's brother, Tenskwatawa, was also known as the Prophet.

He preached to the Indians that he was a prophet who was like an open door to the Master of All Life. Indians from all over the territory came to hear Tenskwatawa speak.

Tenskwatawa joined Tecumseh in uniting the Indians. He and Tecumseh began to convince thousands of Indians they could save their land by joining together.

Tenskwatawa Darkens the Sky

William Henry Harrison was the U.S. governor of the Indiana Territory. He worried about Tenskwatawa's growing number of followers. Harrison did not believe that Tenskwatawa was a prophet. Harrison said that if Tenskwatawa were really a prophet, he should "cause the sun to stand still."

Soon after Harrison's challenge, Tenskwatawa gathered his followers at the Shawnee settlement in Greenville, Ohio. Tenskwatawa had learned that an eclipse of the sun was going to occur. In the morning of June 16, 1806, Tenskwatawa asked the Master of All Life to darken the sky. A full solar eclipse occurred as the Moon passed between the Sun and Earth. The event awed Tenskwatawa's followers. They placed more faith in him and gave him more power. Harrison was not impressed.

Tecumseh and Tenskwatawa set up a new village along the Tippecanoe River in Indiana. They called the village Prophetstown. Tecumseh welcomed visitors from many Indian nations. The brothers preached unity to the growing band of followers. Tecumseh also traveled by horse to recruit more people to his cause. Warriors from the Kickapoo, the Miami, the Creek, the Choctaw, and other tribes joined Tecumseh and Tenskwatawa.

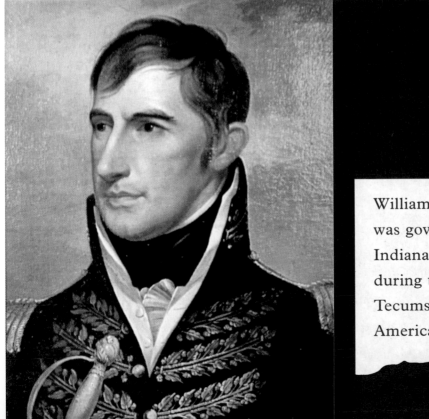

William Henry Harrison was governor of the Indiana Territory during the time Tecumseh was uniting American Indians.

The Land Is Ours

In 1810, Governor Harrison invited Tenskwatawa to Vincennes, Indiana. Harrison was worried about the number of Indians coming to Prophetstown. Tecumseh visited Harrison in Tenskwatawa's place. Tecumseh brought 80 canoes carrying 400 Indians. He told Harrison that the U.S. treaties were unfair. Tecumseh said individual tribes could not legally sell land to the U.S. government because the land belonged to everyone.

Tecumseh's voice and manner impressed U.S. soldiers at Vincennes. Harrison later wrote that Tecumseh was a genius. "If it were not for the [nearness] of the United States, he would perhaps be

At a meeting in 1810, Tecumseh and Harrison almost got into a fight. The men could not agree about who should control the land.

Who Owns the Land?

When meeting Governor William Henry Harrison, Tecumseh said, "[The land] belongs to all for the use of each. For no [tribe] has a right to sell [the land], even to each other, much less to strangers—those who want all and will not do with less."

the founder of an Empire that would rival in glory [the Aztecs in] Mexico or [the Incas in] Peru."

Tecumseh negotiated with dignity and honor, but he could not convince Harrison to return any land. After exchanging angry words that almost resulted in a fight, the two men parted without an agreement about land.

In 1811, Tecumseh wanted to encourage more Indians to fight against the settlers. He planned to leave Prophetstown and bring new warriors to fight. He warned his brother not to battle Harrison while he was gone. If Harrison attacked, he might destroy the unity movement. Tenskwatawa agreed, but after Tecumseh left, Tenskwatawa disobeyed his brother.

The Battle of Tippecanoe

When Tecumseh left, Harrison decided to attack Prophetstown with about 1,000 men. He wanted to destroy the town and calm U.S. fears that the Indians might unite. He believed it was better to attack while Tecumseh was away than to wait for him to return with even more warriors.

The Prophet told his warriors to attack Harrison's army before it could attack them. He promised to protect his warriors with special magic that would make the U.S. Army's bullets useless.

On the night of November 7, 1811, the Battle of Tippecanoe began. Harrison's army attacked the Indians of Prophetstown, and many soldiers were killed. The Indians attacked in turn, but the soldiers were able to beat back the Indians. The army finally defeated the warriors and later burned down Prophetstown. Harrison ordered the planted crops destroyed so the Indians would have no food for the winter. This destruction of crops further weakened Tenskwatawa's people. Tenskwatawa ran away when it was clear his warriors had lost the battle.

Not All Indians Joined Tecumseh

Many, but not all, Indian nations joined Tecumseh's unity movement. Some believed it was best to get along with white settlers. Some Indians believed they should avoid white people completely. The Chickasaw and other nations were respectful of Tecumseh and his message but did not join his movement. Other nations were not so polite. Choctaw chief Pushmataha, pictured below, called Tecumseh a troublemaker.

About 150 soldiers and 40 Indian warriors died during the Battle of Tippecanoe. Because the warriors retreated from the battlefield, Harrison's force claimed victory at the battle.

The Battle of Tippecanoe was a turning point for Tecumseh's unity movement. Many of Tecumseh's followers ran away. Tenskwatawa's remaining followers found him and took him prisoner. They said he was a liar because his magic had not worked.

The Shawnee and other American Indians lost the Battle of Tippecanoe. Tenskwatawa lost much of his influence with the Indians, and Tecumseh sent his brother away after the battle.

Harrison's Political Career

William Henry Harrison was governor of the Indiana Territory when he first met Tecumseh. As governor, Harrison protected white settlers from American Indians. He led troops into the Battle of Tippecanoe and was a U.S. Army general during the War of 1812.

In 1840, Harrison was elected U.S. president. His campaign slogan was "Tippecanoe and Tyler, too." "Tippecanoe" reminded people of his role in the Battle of Tippecanoe. "Tyler" referred to John Tyler, his vice president. On April 4, 1841, Harrison died of pneumonia, just one month after he took office. Tyler became the next president.

When Tecumseh returned from his recruiting journey, he was furious with his brother. Some of the warriors wanted to kill Tenskwatawa. Instead, Tecumseh sent his brother away and would not let him live with their followers. Tenskwatawa wandered from village to village until finally settling in Kansas. He died there in 1836. Tecumseh believed Tenskwatawa's actions had ruined any hope of uniting the Indian nations.

Chapter Five

War with the United States

In the early 1800s, the United States had a poor relationship with Great Britain. British ships stopped U.S. ships at sea, and British sailors forced U.S. sailors to work on British ships. This practice was called impressment. Great Britain impressed sailors to fight a war against France in Europe. On the frontier, the British gave guns, bullets, and food to American Indians and encouraged them to attack U.S. settlers. These British actions angered Americans.

In 1810, several men from southern farming states and the West were elected to Congress. They were called War Hawks because they thought war with Great Britain would be a good idea. They saw their farmers' crops unsold because British ships stopped ships carrying crops to France and other countries.

The War Hawks hoped a war with Great Britain could solve the problems between the two

In the early 1800s, British naval ships made sure no U.S. ships tried to take trade goods to France. This blockade was one cause of war between Great Britain and the United States.

countries. A war also might allow the United States to drive the British from Canada and join it to the United States. On June 18, 1812, Congress declared war on Great Britain and began the War of 1812.

Tecumseh Joins the British Forces

Tecumseh wanted the British to win the war. He hoped the British would sign a treaty with him to establish a nation for Indians. He gathered a large force of warriors who joined British General Isaac Brock in Ontario, Canada. The two men had similar fighting styles and quickly became friends.

In August 1812, Tecumseh and Brock led their men to Fort Detroit in present-day Michigan. U.S. Army General William Hull was in command of the fort. He gave up without a fight after the British fired several cannonballs into the fort. After the U.S. defeat, more American Indians began to join the British forces.

During the fall of 1812 and winter of 1813, Tecumseh's warriors fought throughout the Northwest Territory. In the spring of 1813,

Tecumseh and the Northwest Territory, 1814

CANADA

ONTARIO

MINNESOTA

Lake Superior

WISCONSIN

Lake Huron

Lake Michigan

MICHIGAN

Thames River

THAMES RIVER

FORT DETROIT

• Moraviantown

FALLEN TIMBERS

Lake Erie

Lake Ontario

FORT MEIGS

Maumee River

OHIO

TIPPECANOE

ILLINOIS

Tippecanoe River

• Greenville

INDIANA

• Vincennes

UNITED STATES

LEGEND

United States

Northwest Territory

✳ Battle Site

• City

SCALE
Miles

| 0 | 50 | 100 | 150 | 200 |

| 0 | 50 | 100 | 150 | 200 |

Kilometers

Tecumseh arrived at Fort Malden near the town of Amherstburg, Ontario. Henry Procter was the British commanding general. Procter agreed to work with Tecumseh, but the Shawnee chief did not like Procter. This general was cautious and slow.

The Battle of Fort Meigs

In April 1813, Procter and Tecumseh led their men against William Henry Harrison at Fort Meigs, Ohio. The British soldiers and Tecumseh's warriors attacked fiercely. They killed many men arriving to defend the fort and captured more than 550 soldiers. They took the Americans to a camp, but Tecumseh rode back a different way. While he was gone, his warriors tortured and killed many prisoners. When Tecumseh returned, he stopped the torture. He was angry at Procter for not stopping it.

Tecumseh and Procter continued to lead attacks on Fort Meigs, but the U.S. soldiers would not surrender. Finally, Tecumseh and Procter gave up and returned to Canada to rest and make plans.

Less than a month later, the British soldiers began to pack. Tecumseh accused his British allies of acting like frightened dogs. He gave an emotional speech calling his warriors to arms. He told the British to leave, but he wanted to stay and fight.

Procter told Tecumseh the U.S. Navy had beaten the British fleet on nearby Lake Erie. Harrison was leading 3,000 men into Canada and soon would cut off the British and Shawnee from their supplies. Procter said his forces had to retreat or be trapped. When Tecumseh learned this news, he agreed to go with Procter and his soldiers. The Indians protected the retreating British.

Tecumseh, on horseback, stopped his own followers from killing and torturing their American prisoners.

Chapter Six

The Panther Disappears

Tecumseh and his band of 600 warriors marched with Procter to the Canadian settlement of Moraviantown. This town was located on the Thames River in Ontario. During the march, more than half of Tecumseh's warriors deserted him. He told many of them to leave if they were not comfortable battling the United States.

Tecumseh asked Procter to let the Indians wait along the road to Detroit. From their hiding places, they could attack Harrison's men. Procter agreed. Tecumseh and his men settled on a ridge near the Thames River.

On October 4, 1813, Tecumseh talked to his followers. He told them the U.S. soldiers would easily defeat the British. He believed he would die in battle. He gave personal items to his closest friends.

On October 4, 1813, Tecumseh spoke to his followers. He told them he believed he would die in the next day's battle.

He asked his warriors to retreat and save themselves if he died in battle.

On the afternoon of October 5, about 1,000 U.S. soldiers on horses attacked the British during what was called the Battle of the Thames River.

Richard Johnson of Kentucky, above, claimed he killed Tecumseh. Historians are unsure about his claim. Running for U.S. vice president in 1836, Johnson's slogan was, "Rumpsey, Dumpsey, Johnson killed Tecumseh."

The British ran to save themselves. General Procter jumped on his horse and escaped.

Harrison's men then moved along the river to battle Tecumseh's men. Tecumseh and his men fought the soldiers hand to hand. While fighting, Tecumseh shouted, "Be brave, be brave." Within half an hour, a soldier shot Tecumseh through the chest, killing him. His warriors quickly retreated.

Tecumseh's Body Disappears

After the Battle of the Thames River, bodies littered the battlefield. The U.S. soldiers were unsure if Tecumseh was among the bodies. They looked for someone dressed like a chief, but Tecumseh had been wearing simple leggings.

What happened to Tecumseh's body is unclear. Some researchers believe Tecumseh's warriors returned after dark and carried their dead leader to a creek. They quickly buried him near the shore. When the warriors returned later to bury Tecumseh properly, his body was gone. The creek probably had flooded and washed away the body.

After the War of 1812, the British retreated into Canada. The U.S. Army and American settlers forced the Shawnee from their lands. No one replaced Tecumseh as a leader. His dreams of a united Indian nation died with him.

The U.S. government forced many Indian nations to settle on reservations farther west. Many Indians ended up in the area of present-day Oklahoma. When oil was discovered on these reservation lands, the government forced the Indians to move again. Many Indian people died from hunger and illness during these forced moves.

The Shawnee Today

Today, about 14,000 Shawnee live mostly in three groups in Oklahoma. Not all of the Shawnee people live on reservations or near their tribal headquarters. Modern Shawnee work and live much like other Americans. Many are doctors, lawyers, teachers, or other workers.

Tecumseh holds a special place in Shawnee tribal memory. He was a brave, merciful chief who died a hero's death trying to save his people's lands. Settlers and soldiers respected him. They passed stories of his bravery to the generations of American citizens moving west. Hundreds of years later, the Shawnee and many other people remember the story of Tecumseh.

Many modern Shawnee, such as this family, live in Oklahoma.

41

TIMELINE

Chronology of Tecumseh's Life

Participates in attacks
on U.S. settlers

Settles Prophetstown with
his brother, the Prophet

Loses at the Battle
of Fallen Timbers

Born in Ohio

Begins tribal unity movement

| 1768 | 1783–1790 | 1794 | 1800 | 1807 | 1808 |

Historical Events

Congress passes a law to end
trade with Great Britain.

42

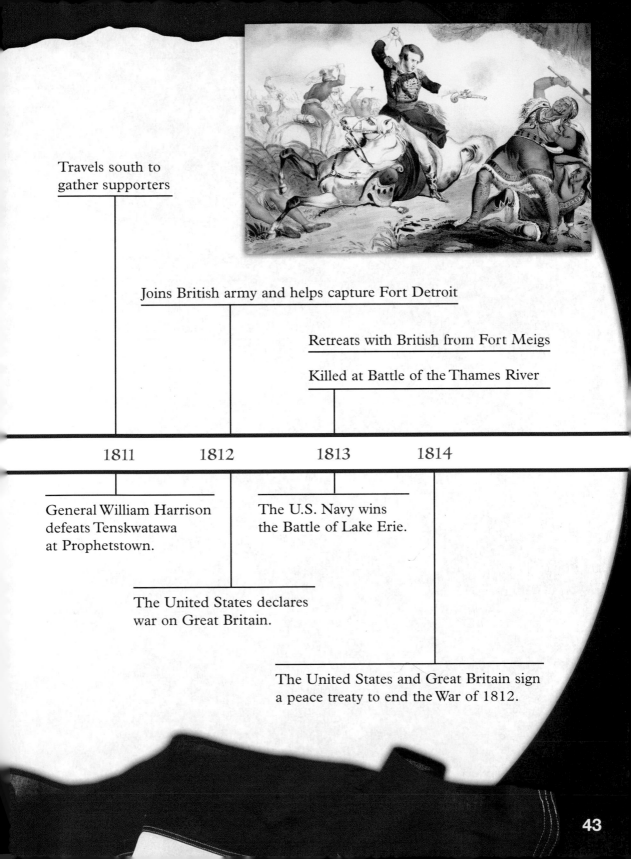

Travels south to gather supporters

Joins British army and helps capture Fort Detroit

Retreats with British from Fort Meigs

Killed at Battle of the Thames River

1811   1812   1813   1814

General William Harrison defeats Tenskwatawa at Prophetstown.

The U.S. Navy wins the Battle of Lake Erie.

The United States declares war on Great Britain.

The United States and Great Britain sign a peace treaty to end the War of 1812.

Glossary

alliance (uh-LYE-uhnss)—a friendly agreement to work together

ally (AL-eye)—a person or country that supports another

clan (KLAN)—a large group of related families

frontier (fruhn-TIHR)—the boundary between settled territory and wilderness

naval (NAY-vuhl)—having to do with a navy or warships

prophet (PROF-it)—someone who claims to speak for a god

reservation (rez-ur-VAY-shuhn)—land set aside by the U.S. government for American Indians to use

treaty (TREE-tee)—a formal agreement between two or more governments or nations

unsoma (oon-SOH-muh)—a good luck charm or special event connected to the birth of Shawnee; an unsoma stays with a Shawnee his or her entire life.

For Further Reading

Fitterer, C. Ann. *Tecumseh: Chief of the Shawnee.* Chanhassen, Minn.: Child's World, 2003.

Koestler-Grack, Rachel A. *Tecumseh, 1768–1813.* American Indian Biographies. Mankato, Minn.: Blue Earth Books, 2003.

Stefoff, Rebecca. *Tecumseh and the Shawnee Confederation.* Library of American Indian History. New York: Facts on File, 1998.

Stefoff, Rebecca. *The War of 1812.* North American Historical Atlases. New York: Benchmark Books, 2001.

Todd, Anne M. *The War of 1812.* America Goes to War. Mankato, Minn.: Capstone Books, 2001.

Places of Interest

Fort Malden National Historic Site of Canada

P.O. Box 38
100 Laird Avenue
Amherstburg, ON N9V 2Z2
Canada

The Battle of the Thames River was fought near this historic site.

Fort Meigs State Memorial

29100 West River Road
Perrysburg, OH 43552

William Henry Harrison built this fort to defend Northwest Ohio and Indiana from Indians and the British during the War of 1812. The fort contains a museum with exhibits that explain the war.

Saline County State Fish and Wildlife Area

85 Glen O. Jones Road
Equality, IL 62934

A life-sized bronze statue of Tecumseh stands at the head of the park's Eagle Mountain-Crest hiking trail.

Tippecanoe Battlefield

State Road 43
North of Lafayette, Indiana
For information, write to
The Tippecanoe County
Historical Association
909 South Street
Lafayette, IN 47901

An interpretive center at the battleground houses a museum.

Internet Sites

Do you want to learn more about Tecumseh?
Visit the FACT HOUND at *http://www.facthound.com*

FACT HOUND can track down many sites to help you.
All the FACT HOUND sites are hand-selected
by Capstone Press editors. FACT HOUND will fetch the best,
most accurate information to answer your questions.

IT IS EASY! IT IS FUN!
1) Go to *http://www.facthound.com*
2) Type in: 0736815562
3) Click on "FETCH IT," and
   FACT HOUND will put you
   on the trail of several helpful links.

You can also search by subject or book title. So, relax
and let our pal FACT HOUND do the research for you!

Index